A Guide to Healthy Relationships for Women with ADHD

Empowering Women for Strong and Healthy Relationships

By

Meghan J. Brooks

Table of Contents

Introduction

Understanding ADHD in Women and its Impact on Relationships

Attention-Deficit/Hyperactivity Disorder (ADHD) is usually connected with kids, yet it influences people, everything being equal, including grown-up women. In any case, ADHD in women frequently goes undiscovered or misconstrued because of its different show contrasted with men and young men. Understanding ADHD in women and its effect on relationships is urgent in creating better and additional satisfying associations.

It, right off the bat, is vital to perceive that ADHD in women might show uniquely in contrast to in men. While hyperactivity is a more noticeable side effect in guys, women will quite often show more inner side effects, like heedlessness, disorder, and impulsivity. These qualities can altogether influence individual relationships , as they can prompt carelessness, trouble with using time productively, and battles in finishing responsibilities.

The effect of ADHD on relationships can change contingent on the seriousness of side effects and individual survival methods. Challenges frequently emerge in regions like correspondence, intimate closeness, and shared liabilities. women with ADHD might battle with viable correspondence, encountering challenges in communicating their necessities, effectively tuning in, or keeping up with the center during discussions. This can prompt mistaken assumptions, disappointment, and diminished intimate association with partners. Moreover, ADHD can cause battles with direction, focusing on tasks, and overseeing liabilities inside the relationship. women with ADHD might battle with putting together family obligations, adjusting work and individual life, and reliably living up to assumptions. This can prompt sensations of overpowering, stress, and burden on the relationship dynamics.

Emotional intimacy is one more viewpoint impacted by ADHD in women. Impulsivity and profound guideline challenges can cause trouble in managing feelings and can prompt extraordinary responses or hasty direction. This can cause strain, errors, and flimsiness inside the relationship. Supporting profound association and cultivating compassion can be especially trying for women with ADHD. It is pivotal to comprehend that the effect of ADHD on relationships isn't an impression of individual deficiency or an absence of responsibility. A chief working issue influences different parts of life, including relationships. Whenever ADHD is perceived and perceived, women can do whatever it may take to deal with its belongings and foster better relationship propensities. Luckily, there are procedures and backing accessible to assist women with ADHD explore relationships effectively. Building mindfulness is vital, as it permits people to perceive their ADHD-related challenges and gives an understanding of their requirements and assets. Successful relational abilities can be created through treatment and relationship schooling, assisting women with putting themselves out there confidently and effectively paying attention to their partners. Laying out sound boundaries, overseeing time really, and looking for help through treatment or training can likewise support adapting to the challenges of ADHD in relationships.

All in all, understanding ADHD in women and its effect on relationships is essential for cultivating better and additional satisfying associations. By perceiving the special ways ADHD appears in women, like negligence, disruption, and impulsivity, we can acquire knowledge about the challenges faced in relationships. Imparting, overseeing liabilities, and sustaining intimate closeness can be areas of trouble for women with ADHD. Nonetheless, with mindfulness, schooling, and backing, women can foster methodologies to explore these challenges and develop satisfying and enduring relationships. It is critical to recollect that ADHD doesn't characterize an individual's worth or capacity for effective relationships, it just requires extra grasping, sympathy, and communication to construct solid and steady associations.

Defining ADHD and its Unique Manifestation in Women

Defining ADHD, or Attention-Deficit/Hyperactivity is urgent to grasp its novel appearance in women. ADHD is a neurodevelopmental problem that influences the cerebrum's chief capabilities, bringing about challenges with consideration, impulsivity, and hyperactivity. While generally connected with young men and men, ADHD is currently perceived as similarly common in women, yet frequently undiscovered or neglected.

What makes the appearance of ADHD in women's novels is how it can vary from the cliché side effects found in guys. Women with ADHD might show less hyperactive ways of behaving, prompting their challenges to be misjudged or excused. All things considered, they will quite often show more incorporated side effects, portrayed by trouble with association, using time effectively, and keeping up with the center. women with ADHD frequently battle with chief working abilities, like preparation, focusing on, and starting errands. They might feel overpowered by regular obligations, experience neglect, and battle with using time productively. Furthermore, women with ADHD might wrestle with profound guidelines, confronting emotional episodes, elevated awareness, and trouble overseeing pressure. The appearance of ADHD in women can likewise impact their relationships. They might encounter challenges with correspondence, as their battles with centering and impulsivity can affect undivided attention and putting themselves out there successfully. These challenges can prompt false impressions and clashes inside private and expert relationships.

Besides, women with ADHD might confront extra cultural strain to adjust to cultural assumptions for association, using time effectively, and profound guidelines. These assumptions can add to deep-seated insecurities, low confidence, and self-question. It is urgent to perceive and comprehend the novel show of ADHD in women to guarantee exact determination and suitable help. Recognizing the particular challenges faced by women considers designated mediations and procedures that can assist them with conquering deterrents and flourishing in different spaces of life.

Recognizing the unmistakable signs of ADHD in women, people, medical care suppliers, and emotionally supportive networks can give the grasping, approval, and assets important to enable and help women with ADHD in dealing with their side effects. Schooling, mindfulness, and early meditation are key in guaranteeing women with ADHD get the fundamental help to lead satisfying lives and assemble sound relationships.

Examining the Challenges Faced in Relationships due to ADHD

Examining the challenges faced in relationships because of ADHD reveals insight into the novel deterrents that people with ADHD might experience inside their relational associations. ADHD, or Attention-Deficit/Hyperactivity Disorder, can influence different parts of relationships, including correspondence, profound guidelines, and in general relationship dynamics. One of the essential challenges comes from hardships with consideration and concentration. People with ADHD might battle to keep up with supported consideration during discussions or exercises with their partners. They might turn out to be quickly flustered or show indiscreet ways of behaving that intrude on the progression of correspondence. This can prompt mistaken assumptions, dissatisfaction, and sensations of being unheard or immaterial.

One more test connected with ADHD in relationships is impulsivity. This impulsivity can appear in imprudent discourse, where people with ADHD might exclaim things disregarding the effect of their words, possibly causing struggle or putting them in a horrible mood. It can likewise add to rash activities, like pursuing hurried choices or taking part in dangerous ways of behaving. These rash inclinations can upset the amiability and strength of relationships. intimate guideline troubles, which are normal in people with ADHD, can likewise introduce challenges inside relationships. Individuals with ADHD might battle to deal with their feelings actually, encountering extreme emotional episodes or trouble controlling displeasure or dissatisfaction. These profound changes can strain relationships and create added pressure or strain.

Furthermore, people with ADHD might confront challenges in overseeing liabilities and keeping up with associations inside relationships. They might battle with errands like family tasks, monetary administration, or sticking to responsibilities and timetables. This can cause strain and lopsidedness inside the relationship, as the non-ADHD partner might feel troubled by a lopsided conveyance of obligations. Misalignment in needs and inspiration can likewise be a test in relationships where ADHD is available. The person with ADHD might experience issues focusing on long-haul objectives or may battle to remain roused and predictable in chasing after shared goals. This misalignment can prompt disappointment and friction between partners who have various assumptions and desires. Critically, these challenges are not outlandish. Perceiving and understanding the effect of ADHD on relationships takes into account proactive systems and mediation to address these hardships. Transparent correspondence, persistence, and sympathy are key in exploring the challenges brought about by ADHD. The two partners can cooperate to foster survival techniques, lay out clear and reasonable assumptions, and offer help in regions where the person with ADHD might require help. Looking for proficient assistance, like couples treatment or ADHD-explicit advising, can likewise give important direction and apparatuses to further developing relationship dynamics. It means quite a bit to move toward these provokes with sympathy and an eagerness to adjust and learn, both exclusively and as a couple.

By recognizing and tending to the challenges presented by ADHD in relationships, couples can develop grasping, persistence, and versatility. With viable correspondence, support, and a cooperative methodology, people with ADHD and their partners can make progress toward areas of strength for building, and satisfying relationships.

Importance of Seeking Support and Strategies for Managing ADHD

Perceiving the importance of seeking support and strategies for managing ADHD is pivotal for people living with this neurodevelopmental problem. ADHD, or Attention-Deficit/Hyperactivity Disorder, influences different parts of life, including scholarly execution, vocational achievement, and individual relationships. Looking for help and carrying out compelling methodologies can fundamentally work on one's capacity to oversee ADHD side effects and upgrade by and large prosperity.

One vital justification for looking for help is to get an exact conclusion. ADHD can frequently go undiscovered or misdiagnosed, prompting challenges in getting it and successfully dealing with its side effects. An expert assessment can give clearness and approval, assisting people with understanding their encounters and accessing fitting assets. With a determination close by, looking for fitting help becomes fundamental. Emotionally supportive networks can incorporate medical care experts, specialists, support gatherings, and friends and family. These people can offer direction, understanding, and reasonable procedures for overseeing ADHD side effects. They can assist people with investigating custom-fitted treatment choices, foster survival techniques, and offer profound help all through the excursion.

Carrying out methodologies for overseeing ADHD enables people to explore everyday difficulties. These systems can incorporate time usage strategies, authoritative apparatuses, and laying out schedules to advance construction and consistency. Creating successful reviews or work propensities, like breaking undertakings into more modest, sensible pieces, using updates and alerts, and carrying out systems for boundary interruptions, can improve efficiency and execution. Looking for help and utilizing techniques for overseeing ADHD additionally adds to working on mindfulness. By grasping one's assets, shortcomings, and triggers, people can foster self-sympathy and self-acknowledgement. This mindfulness encourages a feeling of strengthening, empowering people to proactively address challenges and roll out good improvements in their lives.

Moreover, looking for help and using systems for overseeing ADHD can decidedly affect relationships. Successful communication with partners, relatives, and companions about ADHD can expand understanding and sympathy. Friends and family can figure out how to offer fitting help and facilities to assist people with ADHD flourish. Furthermore, couples or family treatment can give a place of refuge to address relationship challenges connected with ADHD and foster techniques for viable correspondence, compromise, and common help.

Generally, looking for help and executing systems for overseeing ADHD can groundbreakingly affect different everyday issues. It permits people to advance their assets, conquer their difficulties, and lead satisfying and fruitful lives. Through emotionally supportive networks, self-care practices, treatment, and proactive procedures, people with ADHD can develop flexibility, certainty, and a feeling of command over their side effects. It is an excursion of self-revelation and development, empowering people to embrace their one-of-a-kind neuro contrast and flourish in a world that may not necessarily in every case comprehend or oblige their necessities.

Chapter 1

Building Mindfulness and Self-care

Perceiving and Tolerating ADHD Qualities and their Effect on Relationships

Perceiving and tolerating ADHD qualities in relationships include understanding the novel attributes and challenges frequently experienced by people with ADHD. ADHD, or Attention-Deficit/Hyperactivity Disorder is a neurological condition that influences an individual's capacity to control consideration, impulsivity, and hyperactivity. In women, ADHD can introduce contrastingly contrasted with men, frequently appearing as troubles with the inside association, profound guideline, and confidence.

Perceiving ADHD qualities inside oneself requires a legit and non-critical assessment of specific examples and ways of behaving. These may incorporate battling with keeping up with the center, getting quickly flustered, rashness, neglect, trouble with using time productively, and conflicting completion of tasks and responsibilities. Recognizing these attributes is urgent because it permits people to comprehend that these challenges are not private blemishes or character abandons, but rather inborn parts of their neurobiology.

Tolerating ADHD characteristics about relationships includes understanding what they mean for relational dynamics. People with ADHD may unexpectedly fail to remember significant dates or responsibilities, battle to effectively tune in during discussions, or become overpowered by the requests of day-to-day existence. This can prompt errors, disappointment, and sensations of disregard or disappointment for the two partners. By perceiving and tolerating ADHD attributes, people can develop self-compassion and foster successful ways of dealing with hardship or stress to deal with these difficulties. This incorporates looking for help, both from partners and experts, to improve communication and understanding inside relationships.

Perceiving and tolerating ADHD qualities likewise prepares for transparent discussions with partners about the condition and its effect on the relationship. It takes into consideration a mutual perspective of the challenges faced by the person with ADHD and encourages sympathy and tolerance from the partner. This shared acknowledgment and acknowledgment

makes a strong starting point for cooperating to find techniques and facilities that can uphold the relationship and the singular's prosperity. Also, tolerating ADHD qualities helps shift the concentration from fault or dissatisfaction towards finding viable arrangements and looking for proficient direction when required. It empowers people to focus on self-care, for example, carrying out association frameworks, consolidating compelling survival strategies, and overseeing feelings of anxiety. Furthermore, it supports the investigation of treatment choices, like medicine, treatment, or training, that can assist with overseeing ADHD side effects and further develop relationship dynamics.

In outline, perceiving and tolerating ADHD characteristics with regards to relationships is fundamental for both self-understanding and cultivating better, additional satisfying associations. It includes recognizing the effect of ADHD on different parts of life and relationships, considering sympathy, understanding, and proactive strides

towards overseeing challenges and tracking down procedures that help the well-being of the two people included.

Developing Self-Compassion and Embracing Self-Care Practices

Developing self-compassion and embracing self-care practice are fundamental parts of encouraging a solid and satisfying life for women with ADHD. Self-compassion includes treating oneself with generosity, understanding, and acknowledgment, particularly while confronting the novel challenges that accompany ADHD. It is fundamental to recognize that ADHD is not an individual fizzling or shortcoming but rather a neurological condition that influences different parts of day-to-day existence and relationships. embracing self-care practices includes effectively focusing on one's physical, close to home, and mental prosperity. women with ADHD frequently wind up wrecked and depleted because of the requests of day-to-day existence, which can adversely influence their general well-being and relationships. By getting some margin to focus on themselves, ADHD women

can recharge their energy, diminish feelings of anxiety, and improve their capacity to oversee side effects.

Creating self-compassion begins with perceiving and tolerating the effect of ADHD on one's life. It includes supplanting self-judgment and analysis with understanding and compassion. This implies reexamining negative considerations and embracing a kinder internal exchange. Perceiving that slip-ups and misfortunes are essential for the ADHD experience considers self-pardoning and a more certain healthy identity. embracing self-care practices includes a great many methodologies. It includes laying out solid schedules and focusing on exercises that advance physical and mental prosperity. This might incorporate participating in normal activity, eating adjusted and nutritious dinners, and getting adequate tranquil rest. self-care additionally includes defining boundaries and figuring out how to say no when fundamental, as overcommitment can prompt overpowering and burnout.

Notwithstanding actual self-care, intimate and mental self-care are similarly significant. This might include taking part in exercises that give pleasure

and unwinding, like leisure activities, imaginative outlets, or investing energy in nature. Looking for help through treatment, advising, or upholding gatherings can likewise be useful to address personal challenges and foster ways of dealing with stress well defined for ADHD. Rehearsing self-sympathy and self-care advantages the person with ADHD as well as emphatically influences relationships. By dealing with themselves, women with ADHD can more readily oversee side effects, decrease pressure, and work on by and large prosperity. This, thus, improves their ability to take part in better and additional satisfying relationships.

In general, creating self-compassion and embracing self-care practices for women with ADHD is fundamental for building versatility, overseeing side effects, and encouraging an identity worth. A continuous interaction requires persistence, understanding, and a guarantee to focus on one's requirements. By sustaining themselves with generosity and rehearsing self-care, women with ADHD can explore life all the more, develop better relationships, and embrace their novel assets and capacities.

Managing Stress and Enhancing Overall Well-Being

Managing stress and enhancing overall well-being is significant for women with ADHD, as they frequently experience uplifted degrees of stress and may battle with keeping a feeling of equilibrium and congruency in their lives. The remarkable challenges related to ADHD, like hardships with association, using time productively, and keeping up with the center, can add to expanded feelings of anxiety.

To successfully oversee pressure, women with ADHD should foster a diverse methodology that tends to both the physical and profound parts of well-being. This approach might include:

Self-Care Practices: Participating in standard self-care exercises is fundamental for diminishing pressure and advancing by and large prosperity. This can include exercises like activity, getting adequate rest, rehearsing care or reflection, and taking part in leisure activities or exercises that give pleasure and unwinding.

Laying out Practical Objectives and Boundaries: women with ADHD frequently feel overpowered by

various obligations and assumptions. Putting forth practical objectives and focusing on tasks can assist in dealing with focusing by separating them into reasonable pieces. This incorporates making plans for the day, utilizing authoritative instruments or applications, and looking for help from friends and family to assign errands when fundamental.

Time Usage Systems: Using time productively is significant for women with ADHD to forestall feeling overpowered and pushed. Using apparatuses like clocks, schedules, and alerts can assist with organizing time really, guaranteeing that significant tasks and commitments are met without unnecessary tension. Furthermore, laying out schedules and adhering to a steady timetable can give a feeling of steadiness and diminish tension.

Stress Decrease Strategies: Learning and carrying out pressure decrease procedures can altogether work on general prosperity. Profound breathing activities, moderate muscle unwinding, and directed symbolism can assist with decreasing feelings of anxiety at the time. Participating in normal actual activity, like yoga or high-impact exercises, can likewise deliver endorphins and advance a feeling of quiet.

Looking for Help: It is fundamental for women with ADHD to connect for help from friends and family, support gatherings, or emotional wellness experts. Interfacing with other people who comprehend the challenges of ADHD can give a feeling of approval and consolation. Looking for treatment or advice can likewise give apparatuses and systems to overseeing pressure, building adapting abilities, and upgrading general prosperity.

Embracing Self-Sympathy: women with ADHD should develop self-compassion and practice self-acknowledgement. Perceiving that ADHD doesn't characterize their value or capacities is imperative. Praising victories, regardless of how little, and reevaluating mishaps as learning open doors can add to a better mentality and diminish purposeful pressure.

By executing these procedures and focusing on self-care, women with ADHD can oversee pressure and improve their general prosperity. It is critical to recall that finding the right mix of methods might require some experimentation, as what works for one individual may not work for another. By showing restraint toward yourself and looking for the help you want, you can develop a better and

more healthy lifestyle, permitting you to explore the challenges of ADHD with more noteworthy strength and prosperity.

Chapter 2

Effective Communication Strategies

Understanding the Role of Communication in Healthy Relationships

Effective communication strategies are the foundation of any solid relationship, and they hold specific importance for women with ADHD. With ADHD, women frequently battle with keeping up with concentration, impulsivity, and profound guidelines, which can make special challenges in relational collaborations. To cultivate solid and flourishing relationships, it becomes urgent for women with ADHD to handily explore correspondence. Communication in relationships serves a few crucial capabilities. It, right off the bat, permits people to offer their viewpoints, feelings, and necessities to each other. For women with ADHD, effective communication empowers them to express their encounters, including the effect of their side effects, like issues with association or concentration. This sharing of bits of knowledge can advance figuring out, sympathy, and at last, lead to additional humane and steady relationships.

Besides, effective communication assists women with ADHD explore struggles and resolve issues valuably. ADHD side effects can now and again add to mistaken assumptions or increase feelings during conflicts. By using effective communication strategies, like undivided attention, explaining explanations, and utilizing "I" articulations, women with ADHD can put themselves out there plainly and boundary misconceptions. This, thus, cultivates better compromise and guarantees that both parties feel appreciated, esteemed, and regarded. With regards to relationships, communication likewise assumes an imperative part in building trust, encouraging profound closeness, and keeping a feeling of association. women with ADHD might be more deliberate about communicating their adoration, appreciation, and fondness to their partners. Clear and open communication permits them to convey their sentiments really and affectionately, guaranteeing that their partner feels valued and upheld.

It's fundamental for women with ADHD to foster systems that line up with their extraordinary communication style. This might include utilizing visual guides, like schedules or updates, to remain coordinated or utilizing dynamic commitment procedures like rewording or summing up to show understanding during discussions. Moreover, saving committed time for continuous communication can assist with boundary interruptions and advance engaged and significant trade. Without a doubt, successful communication requires mindfulness as well as undivided attention and sympathy for one's partner. women with ADHD can profit from rehearsing undivided attention abilities, for example, keeping in touch, really focusing, and shunning interfering, to establish a climate where communication can flourish. Finally, women with ADHD must perceive that communication is a two-way road. Their partners additionally assume a fundamental part in cultivating solid correspondence.

Empowering open discourse, requesting explanation when required, and being a comprehension of their partner's ADHD challenges can add to a more steady and amicable relationship.

In outline, understanding the job of communication in solid relationships for women with ADHD is imperative for encouraging grasping, settling clashes, building trust, and supporting profound closeness. It includes offering one's viewpoints, feelings, and needs successfully, effectively paying attention to one's partner, and utilizing systems that line up with one's remarkable communication style. Both mindfulness and partner support are pivotal in establishing a climate helpful for open and sympathetic correspondence. With these abilities and methodologies set up, women with ADHD can develop solid and satisfying relationships that blossom with powerful and figuring-out correspondence.

Upgrading Undivided Attention Abilities and Expressing Needs Successfully

Upgrading undivided attention abilities and expressing needs successfully is a critical part of sound relationships for women with ADHD. ADHD can periodically prompt challenges in correspondence, blocking the capacity to completely participate in discussions and successfully convey one's necessities and feelings. In any case, by learning and rehearsing explicit strategies, women with ADHD can extraordinarily further develop their relational abilities and encourage more grounded associations with their partners.

Undivided attention includes completely focusing on and engrossing in what the other individual is talking about, without interruption or interference. For women with ADHD, this can be especially

difficult because of trouble with keeping up with the center. To upgrade undivided attention abilities, it is useful to establish a climate helpful for fixation, boundary-ings outside interruptions like clamor or visual mess. Furthermore, utilizing methods like keeping in touch, gesturing, and giving verbal attestations exhibits dynamic commitment, showing the speaker that their words are being heard and perceived.

Expressing needs successfully is one more imperative part of solid correspondence. Frequently, women with ADHD might experience challenges articulating their necessities plainly, which could prompt false impressions or neglected assumptions. Laying out transparent communication with one's partner is fundamental. It is prescribed to rehearse mindfulness and consider individual necessities before taking part in discussions, taking into account a superior comprehension of what ought to be imparted. Separating complex considerations and feelings into more straightforward, succinct explanations can likewise help with powerful articulation.

Moreover, utilizing explicit models and giving settings can assist with explaining needs and

guarantee that the expected message is precisely passed on. Utilizing "I" proclamations, for example, "I feel" or "I want," assists with taking responsibility for feelings and abstains from accusing the partner, encouraging a more cooperative and conscious conversation. Notwithstanding undivided attention and clear articulation, it is essential to be aware of time. Tracking down the right second to start a discussion can incredibly impact its result. Choosing when the two partners are quiet and open can upgrade the possibilities of effective communication. If interruptions or overpowering feelings emerge during the discussion, it is significant to know about them and recommend having some time off to refocus before continuing the conversation. Lastly, practice and persistence are critical.

Creating undivided attention abilities and expressing needs successfully may take time and exertion. It is vital to keep a development outlook and be empathetic with yourself in the meantime. Looking for help from a specialist or ADHD mentor who has some expertise in relational abilities can likewise be useful in leveling up these skills.

At last, by upgrading their undivided attention abilities and expressing their needs actually, women with ADHD can develop better and additional satisfying relationships. Successful communication considers better grasping, intimate association, and the shared fulfillment of necessities between partners. It makes ready for expanded compassion, participation, and generally speaking relationship fulfillment, upgrading the establishment for a solid and enduring bond.

Navigating Conflict Resolution and Promoting Constructive Conversations

Navigating conflict resolution and promoting constructive conversations can be especially moving for women with ADHD because of the exceptional way ADHD influences their communication and profound guidelines. In any case, by creating powerful techniques, defeating these snags and cultivating better relationships is conceivable.

First and foremost, it is vital to perceive and grasp the effect of ADHD on correspondence. ADHD can add to indiscreet responses, trouble keeping up with consideration during discussions, and a propensity to hinder or blabber. By recognizing these difficulties, women with ADHD can effectively pursue further developing their relational abilities. One key system is rehearsing undivided attention. This includes concentrating entirely on the speaker, keeping in touch, and utilizing verbal and nonverbal prompts to show interest. Undivided attention assists with upgrading understanding and sympathy, which are essential for settling clashes and building more grounded associations. Another significant viewpoint is offering viewpoints and feelings. women with ADHD might find it supportive to coordinate their thoughts ahead of time and express them concisely to guarantee clearness. It can likewise be valuable to delay and enjoy reprieves when expected to abstain from becoming overpowered during extraordinary discussions.

In compromise, advancing a valuable and conscious atmosphere is vital. This can be accomplished by zeroing in on the main thing as opposed to individual assaults, utilizing "I" articulations to communicate sentiments and discernments, and effectively looking to split the difference or shared conviction. Women with ADHD might find it valuable to lay out standard procedures for conversations to guarantee that all gatherings feel appreciated and regarded. Dealing with feelings during clashes is another fundamental angle. ADHD can uplift intimate responsiveness and impulsivity, making it trying to direct feelings during warmed conversations.

Methods like profound breathing, careful consciousness of feelings, and enjoying reprieves to quiet down can be compelling in advancing intimate guidelines and forestalling rash responses.

Moreover, it is essential to be available to input and ready to apologize or offer to set things right when important. Getting a sense of ownership of one's activities and understanding the effect of ADHD on relationship dynamics can encourage understanding and advance compromise. Looking for proficient assistance, for example, couples advising or treatment explicitly centered around ADHD and relationships, can likewise give significant direction and back in exploring compromise. The inclusion of an unbiased outsider can assist with working with open and valuable discussions, taking into consideration a more profound comprehension of one another's viewpoints and necessities.

In rundown, navigating conflict resolution and promoting constructive conversations for women with ADHD requires mindfulness, undivided attention, successful articulation of contemplations and feelings, laying out standard procedures, dealing with feelings, and looking for proficient help when required. By utilizing these techniques, women with ADHD can improve their relational abilities and fabricate better, additional satisfying relationships.

Chapter 3

Adjusting Liabilities and Needs

Coordinating Tasks and Time Usage Procedures

Sorting out tasks and overseeing time really can be especially moving for women with ADHD because of the intrinsic hardships in keeping up with the center, focusing on errands, and overseeing impulsivity. Be that as it may, with the right systems and procedures, it is feasible to defeat these challenges and develop a more coordinated and organized way to deal with day-to-day existence.

Laying out Needs: women with ADHD can benefit extraordinarily from defining clear boundaries. By recognizing the main errands or objectives, it becomes simpler to in like manner dispense time and consideration. Making a daily agenda or utilizing an organizer can be useful in outwardly sorting out errands and it is neglected to not guarantee anything.

Breaking Undertakings into Reasonable Pieces: Enormous or complex errands can be overpowering

for people with ADHD. Separating them into more modest, more sensible advances can cause them to feel more achievable. This interaction likewise considers pride as each step is finished, giving further inspiration to continue onward.

Using Time-Impeding Procedures: Time-hindering includes assigning explicit time allotments for various exercises or errands. By making an organized timetable, women with ADHD can more readily deal with their time and remain focused. It is vital to be practical while assessing the time required for each undertaking and work in support to represent possible interruptions or unanticipated conditions.

Boundarying Interruptions: Interruptions can essentially wreck efficiency and use time effectively. Women with ADHD can profit from establishing a climate that boundaries expected interruptions. This might include eliminating or diminishing visual and hearable interruptions, like switching off notices on electronic gadgets, tracking down a tranquil work area, or utilizing sound-blocking earphones.

Using Computerized Devices and Applications: Innovation can be a significant partner in task association and using time productively. Various

applications and instruments are planned explicitly for people with ADHD, offering dynamics like updates, clocks, and task global positioning frameworks. This computerized help can give design, backing, and suggestions to assist with keeping focused and overseeing time.

Carrying out Schedules and Customs: Laying out steady schedules and ceremonies can assist people with ADHD and foster a feeling of design and consistency. This can incorporate making a morning schedule, setting assigned times for explicit exercises (e.g., workout, dinner prep), and executing a predictable sleep schedule. Schedules give a system for overseeing time while diminishing choice weariness and potential for complication.

Looking for Responsibility and Backing: Having a responsible partner or emotionally supportive network can incredibly upgrade task association and use time effectively. This can be confided in a companion, relative, or even an expert mentor or specialist. Sharing objectives, progress, and challenges with another person gives a feeling of outside responsibility, inspiration, and direction.

Consolidating Obvious Signs and Updates: women with ADHD frequently benefit from viewable

signals to provoke task finish and help in using time productively. This might incorporate utilizing sticky notes, variety-coded schedules, or visual clocks to outwardly address cutoff times and periods. Visual updates can act as accommodating prompts to keep on track and on time.

Rehearsing self-compassion and Adaptability: women with ADHD should rehearse self-sympathy and comprehend that overseeing errands and time may not generally work out as expected. Being adaptable and adjusting procedures depending on the situation is vital to keeping up with inspiration and staying away from sensations of disappointment or overpowering. Embracing a development outlook and perceiving progress, even in little advances, can assist with developing flexibility and proceeding with progress.

By executing these procedures and strategies for task association and using time effectively, women with ADHD can oversee their timetables, lessen pressure, and at last flourish in their own proficient lives. Keep in mind that it's an excursion, and with persistence and tolerance, a more coordinated and useful lifestyle can be accomplished.

Setting Boundaries and Delegating Tasks within Relationships

Setting boundaries and delegating tasks within relationships is a vital part of keeping up with solid and adjusted dynamics, especially for women with ADHD. Because of the special challenges and attributes related to ADHD, for example, trouble focusing on and overseeing time, it becomes fundamental to lay out clear boundaries and delegate tasks. Setting boundaries includes characterizing and imparting boundaries on what is satisfactory or agreeable in a relationship. For women with ADHD, this can mean plainly articulating their necessities, boundaries, and assumptions to their partner, friends, and family. It permits people to safeguard their prosperity, protect their energy, and forestall overpowering circumstances that might fuel ADHD side effects.

Designating undertakings is firmly associated with defining boundaries. It includes allocating explicit obligations and sharing the responsibility inside the relationship. By designating undertakings, women with ADHD can deal with their significant

investment while likewise cultivating a feeling of equity and cooperation. task can include examining and dispensing family errands, childcare obligations, or even dynamic undertakings. With regards to assigning errands in relationships, women with ADHD actually must discuss transparently and sincerely with their partners. This guarantees that the two people have a reasonable comprehension of one another's assets, shortcomings, and capacities. By isolating errands in light of every individual's range of abilities and boundaries, it becomes more straightforward to deal with the requests of day-to-day existence.

Viable designation additionally requires trust and open correspondence. women with ADHD ought to feel open to communicating their necessities and boundaries, while their partner seeks to be responsive and able to help them in dealing with their side effects. It might very well be useful to lay out normal registrations to examine task progress, change liabilities depending on the situation, and address any challenges that might emerge. Moreover, using apparatuses and techniques can extraordinarily help with defining boundaries and designating tasks. This can incorporate making

plans, utilizing updates or clocks, and using hierarchical applications or apparatuses. Separating undertakings into more modest, reasonable advances can likewise make them not so overwhelming but rather more feasible. Keep in mind that defining boundaries and designating undertakings inside relationships isn't tied in with evading liabilities, but rather about establishing a steady and adjusted climate that recognizes and obliges the challenges presented by ADHD. By imparting reality, dispersing tasks, and respecting each other's necessities, women with ADHD can develop better relationships, decrease pressure, and better deal with their side effects, prompting more noteworthy generally speaking well-being for them as well as their friends and family.

Laying Out the Solid Balance between Serious and Fun Activities and Staying Away from Overpower

Laying out a solid balance between serious and fun activities is a pivotal perspective for people with ADHD, especially women, to focus on. ADHD can bring remarkable challenges in overseeing liabilities

and remaining coordinated, which might prompt overpowering sentiments in both expert and individual circles. To stay away from this overpower and make an agreeable balance, creating viable strategies is fundamental.

The most vital phase in laying out a sound balance between fun and serious activities is perceiving the significance of setting practical assumptions. Understanding one's constraints and recognizing that it is OK to now and again take on fewer responsibilities can radically diminish pressure and forestall burnout. women with ADHD can profit from recognizing their needs and zeroing in on the key regions where their significant investment ought to be designated. This incorporates perceiving the meaning of self-care and guaranteeing that individual well-being isn't dismissed.

Time usage assumes a basic part in accomplishing a balance between serious and fun activities. Using viable devices like timetables, schedules, and updates can support putting together undertakings and cutoff times. Separating enormous tasks into more modest, reasonable advances can be useful in forestalling, tarrying, and feeling overpowered. Furthermore, making an organized schedule that

consolidates customary breaks and time for unwinding can further develop concentration and efficiency while lessening sensations of stress. boundaries are one more crucial part of laying out the balance between serious and fun activities. Figuring out how to say 'no' when important and defining clear boundaries can assist women with ADHD keep a good overall arrangement between work and individual life. This includes focusing on self-care exercises, like activities, side interests, and investing quality energy with friends and family. Conveying these boundaries to managers, associates, and relatives can encourage understanding and backing.

In addition, looking for help and designating undertakings can lighten the weight of overseeing everything alone. Women with ADHD can consider teaming up with associates, examining responsibility changes, or looking for help from loved ones for family obligations. This common exertion can ease the burden and make more space for unwinding and individual satisfaction.

Women with ADHD need to be aware of their energy levels and enjoy standard reprieves over the day. Participating in exercises that advance

unwinding and stress decrease, like contemplation, profound breathing activities, or participating in side interests, can assist with re-energizing the brain and forestall mental weakness.

In conclusion, looking for proficient assistance and using accessible assets is essential for keeping up with the balance between fun and serious activities. Interfacing with specialists, ADHD mentors, or care groups explicitly cooked towards women with ADHD can give important direction, survival methods, and a feeling of the local area. These assets can offer customized exhortation and help with exploring the extraordinary challenges faced by women with ADHD in adjusting to work and individual life.

By carrying out these procedures and focusing on self-care, women with ADHD can lay out a better balance between fun and serious activities, diminishing overpowering and accomplishing a more prominent feeling of satisfaction in both expert and special goals. It is essential to recall that finding the right equilibrium is a nonstop excursion, and adaptability and self-sympathy are critical. With time, practice, and continuous help, women with ADHD can effectively explore their day-to-day

obligations while likewise partaking in a satisfying individual life.

Chapter 4

Nurturing Emotional Intimacy and Connection

Investigating the Importance of Emotional Intimacy in Relationships

Emotional intimacy assumes a fundamental part in cultivating sound and satisfying relationships for women with ADHD. It includes making an emotional intimacy association and understanding with your partner, which can improve trust, correspondence, and by and large relationship fulfillment.

For women with ADHD, intimacy can be especially critical as the challenges related to ADHD can at times make it hard to communicate feelings and interface on a more profound level. This can incorporate battles with intimate guidelines, impulsivity, and trouble in perceiving and figuring out one's feelings. Building emotional intimacy includes different viewpoints. It, right off the bat, requires mindfulness and self-reflection, as it is vital to comprehend and acknowledge one's intimate

encounters before having the option to impart them to a partner. This might include perceiving examples, triggers, and qualities connected with ADHD side effects.

Relational abilities play a key part in cultivating intimate closeness. women with ADHD might confront challenges communicating their feelings or considerations reasonably and succinctly. Thus, it is essential to rehearse undivided attention and viable communication procedures, like utilizing "I" articulations and communicating needs and sentiments transparently. This empowers the two partners to feel appreciated, comprehended, and approved, advancing a more emotionally intimate association.

Overseeing impulsivity is another region that adds to intimate closeness. ADHD can now and again prompt hasty responses or ways of behaving, which might upset the foundation of profound closeness. By creating methodologies to oversee impulsivity, for example, stopping and reflecting before answering, women with ADHD can encourage a climate of intimate well-being and soundness in their relationships.

Also, creating sympathy and intimate attunement is key to building profound closeness. This includes effectively paying attention to and attempting to figure out your partner's feelings, viewpoints, and necessities. Women with ADHD can develop these abilities by rehearsing dynamic commitment, posing unconditional inquiries, and exhibiting sympathy and empathy. Making a protected and steady space for profound articulation is fundamental. The two partners ought to feel open to sharing their weaknesses, fears, and delights unafraid of judgment or dismissal. This incorporates approving each other's feelings and giving consolation and backing when required. intimate closeness likewise requires continuous exertion and upkeep. It is vital to focus on quality time together, take part in exercises that advance intimate association and holding, and consistently check in with one another on a profound level.

By exploring and focusing on the importance of emotional intimacy, women with ADHD can develop further associations with their partners, generally improving relationship fulfillment and cultivating a feeling of profound security and satisfaction.

Overseeing Impulsivity and Intimate Guideline

Overseeing impulsivity and intimate guidelines can be especially trying for women with ADHD. Impulsivity alludes to following up without much forethought disregarding the outcomes, which can prompt unfortunate direction and stressed relationships. Profound guidelines, then again, include successfully overseeing and communicating feelings in a sound and controlled way.

To address these troubles, women with ADHD should foster techniques that advance mindfulness and poise. One compelling methodology is to rehearse care procedures, which include zeroing in on the current second and noticing feelings without judgment. This aids in perceiving rash contemplations or profound triggers, permitting people to stop and consider their reactions before responding hastily. Close by care, creating solid survival techniques can uphold profound guidelines. Taking part in customary actual activity, keeping a decent eating routine, and getting adequate tranquil rest can emphatically affect profound prosperity. Furthermore, rehearsing pressure decreases

strategies like profound breathing activities, reflection, or partaking in quieting exercises like yoga or craftsmanship can be useful.

Compelling relational abilities likewise assume a key part in overseeing impulsivity and intimate guidelines. Carving out an opportunity to listen effectively and Reinforcing association through sympathy, approval, and dynamic commitment

Reinforcing association through sympathy, approval, and dynamic commitment is a critical part of building and keeping up with sound relationships for women with ADHD. Sympathy plays an essential part in encouraging comprehension and profound closeness. It includes placing yourself in the shoes of your partner or adored one, and attempting to get a handle on their point of view, feelings, and encounters. For women with ADHD, sympathy is vital to perceiving and recognizing the moves they face because of their condition. By showing compassion, partners can make a protected and steady space where women with ADHD feel appreciated, approved, and acknowledged for what their identity is.

Approval is similarly significant in cultivating association. Frequently, women with ADHD might

experience trouble in exploring everyday errands, overseeing time, or remaining coordinated. Approving their encounters and feelings assists them with feeling comprehended and appreciated. This includes recognizing their endeavors, perceiving their assets, and reevaluating challenges as any open doors for development. Approval supports their confidence and develops a feeling of having a place inside the relationship.

Dynamic commitment alludes to effectively partaking and putting resources into the relationship. It includes being available and mindful, staying away from interruptions, and effectively partaking in discussions and exercises. For women with ADHD, dynamic commitment can be especially difficult because of troubles with consideration and impulsivity. Notwithstanding, by intentionally rehearsing undivided attention, getting clarification on some things, and showing veritable interest and contribution, partners can make areas of strength for association and closeness. Dynamic commitment additionally incorporates effectively looking for ways of supporting and grasping the exceptional requirements and battles of women with ADHD,

like going to instructive studios or treatment meetings together.

By consolidating sympathy, approval, and dynamic commitment to relationships, partners can encourage a more profound comprehension and association with women who have ADHD. This advances a climate of trust, backing, and regard, where the two people feel esteemed and appreciated. It takes into consideration transparent correspondence, taking into consideration the investigation of savvy fixes, and successful critical thinking. Eventually, by focusing on these components, relationships can flourish and prosper, empowering women with ADHD to feel seen, comprehended, and cherished.

Chapter 5

Improving Relationship Dynamics

Figuring out the Effect of ADHD on Relationship Dynamics

ADHD (Attention-Deficit/Hyperactivity) is a neurodevelopmental condition that influences kids and grown-ups. While it is frequently connected with challenges in focus, impulsivity, and hyperactivity, it can likewise essentially affect relationship dynamics.

One critical part of ADHD is trouble with leader capabilities, which are mental cycles liable for arranging, sorting out, and overseeing undertakings. This can make challenges in relationships as people with ADHD might battle with keeping plans, remaining coordinated, and living up to assumptions. For instance, distraction, irregularity, and trouble finishing jobs can prompt disappointment and miscommunication inside an organization.

Mindlessness, one more typical side effect of ADHD, can influence the capacity to listen mindfully and focus on others. This can bring about false impressions, as partners would feel overlooked or unheard. Moreover, an imprudent way of behaving can appear in relationship dynamics, prompting rash decisions or intruding on discussions, which can be problematic and cause strain in a relationship. ADHD can likewise impact intimate guidelines. Individuals with ADHD might encounter uplifted intimate responsiveness, state of mind swings, and anxiety. This profound rollercoaster can influence the general air of a relationship and make it more testing to explore clashes and conflicts.

In addition, the impacts of ADHD can stretch out past the person with the condition. partners might take on extra obligations and feel overpowered, prompting sensations of hatred or lopsidedness in the relationship. This can put pressure on and strain the intimate association between partners. It is vital to take note that understanding the effect of ADHD on relationship dynamics isn't tied in with appointing fault or rationalizing, but rather acquiring knowledge into the particular provokes that emerge and tracking down systems to address them. Open and successful communication becomes significant in exploring these difficulties.

Backing, training, and compassion are fundamental for the two partners in a relationship impacted by ADHD. Finding out about ADHD together can encourage grasping, empathy, and tolerance. It is significant for the non-ADHD partner to perceive that ADHD is certainly not a decision or a personal defect but a neurobiological condition that needs help and understanding. Looking for proficient assistance, like couples treatment or individual treatment, can help tend to the effect of ADHD on relationship dynamics. Treatment can give devices and methods to further develop correspondence, oversee pressure, and track down ways of supporting each other in exploring the challenges of ADHD.

Keep in mind, that with persistence, understanding, and an eagerness to cooperate, it is feasible to fabricate solid and satisfying relationships even within the sight of ADHD. By recognizing and tending to the particular challenges that ADHD presents, partners can establish a climate of help, compassion, and shared development. With powerful systems and continuous correspondence, developing sound and flourishing relationships despite the effect of ADHD is conceivable.

Exploring Strategies for Promoting Equality and Collaboration

Exploring strategies for promoting equality and collaboration for women with ADHD includes establishing a climate where the two partners are esteemed and have an equivalent say in the relationship dynamics. ADHD can present challenges in keeping up with equilibrium and decency, yet with deliberate endeavors, cultivating a cooperative and equivalent partnership is conceivable.

One powerful system is transparent correspondence. women with ADHD can communicate their necessities, difficulties, and qualities to their partners, cultivating understanding and compassion. In like manner, partners are urged to effectively tune in, approve, and support their cherished one with ADHD. This takes into consideration a common comprehension of one another's viewpoints, encouraging a feeling of balance.

Setting clear and fair assumptions is another basic methodology. It includes examining liabilities, jobs, and undertakings inside the relationship transparently. Thus, women with ADHD can advocate for them and guarantee they are not troubled by an unjust appropriation of obligations. partners can cooperate to find an equilibrium that obliges ADHD-related challenges while advancing coordinated effort and decency.

Establishing a strong and organized climate is likewise significant. women with ADHD might profit from obvious prompts, updates, and coordinated frameworks that assist with dealing with their regular routines. Cooperatively creating frameworks that work for the two partners can ease the weight exclusively put on the person with ADHD while advancing shared liability and joint effort.

Normal registrations and assessments can likewise be useful in advancing fairness and coordinated effort. This includes continuous conversations to survey how well the methodologies and frameworks are working and make fundamental changes depending on the situation. By routinely assessing and changing, the two partners can guarantee that the relationship stays fair, adjusted, and strong.

Also, rehearsing tolerance and understanding is critical. women with ADHD might confront exceptional challenges concerning using time effectively, concentration, and impulsivity. partners can cultivate balance and cooperation by keeping up with tolerance, forgoing judgment, and offering support during snapshots of trouble. This assists with making a safe and non-critical space where the two partners feel good and are enabled to add to the relationship effectively.

Finally, looking for proficient direction and support can be priceless. Couples treatment or ADHD-explicit directing can give an organized climate to tending to difficulties, upgrading relational abilities, and investigating procedures for advancing balance and cooperation. Proficient assistance offers direction custom-made to the particular dynamics of the relationship and the challenges related to ADHD, empowering the two partners to develop and flourish together.

By and large, exploring strategies for promoting equality and collaboration for women with ADHD involves open communication, setting clear assumptions, establishing a steady climate, customary assessments, tolerance, and looking for proficient assistance when required. By carrying out these methodologies, couples can explore the intricacies of ADHD together, encouraging a relationship that is based on common regard, understanding, and joint effort.

Addressing Common Relationship Challenges and Finding Solutions

Women with ADHD frequently face remarkable challenges in keeping up with solid and satisfying relationships. To address these challenges and find viable arrangements, vital to comprehend the particular hardships that can emerge. Some normal relationship challenges that women with ADHD might experience incorporate communication troubles, neglect or disorder, impulsivity, and trouble with using time productively.

Powerful communication is a critical part of any fruitful relationship, yet for women with ADHD, it tends to be especially challenging. They might battle with undivided attention, communicating their requirements and feelings obviously, or overseeing struggle in a useful way. Tracking down methodologies to upgrade relational abilities, like creating undivided attention procedures or learning powerful compromise techniques, can extraordinarily further develop relationship dynamics. Neglect and disruption can likewise present huge challenges in relationships. women with ADHD might battle with recollecting significant tasks, arrangements, or responsibilities. This can prompt dissatisfaction and false impressions with partners who might feel disregarded or irrelevant. Carrying out down-to-earth systems, like utilizing schedules, updates, or making schedules, can assist with tending to these challenges and work on general association and unwavering quality.

Impulsivity is one more typical trouble for women with ADHD. They might act or talk automatically, prompting circumstances that might strain relationships. Figuring out how to oversee impulsivity through methods, for example, stopping before answering, rehearsing self-reflection, and creating motivation control systems can be instrumental in encouraging better cooperation inside relationships.

Using time productively can likewise be a huge wellspring of stress and dissatisfaction for women with ADHD. Troubles in focusing on tasks, assessing time precisely, and overseeing cutoff times can put pressure on relationships. Executing compelling time usage strategies, like breaking errands into more modest and reasonable advances, using visual guides or clocks, and laying out practical objectives, can assist with easing these challenges and advance a feeling of construction and equilibrium inside the relationship.

To address these normal relationship challenges, women with ADHD genuinely must effectively look for arrangements and backing. This can include looking for proficient assistance from advisors spending significant time in ADHD or couples directing, going to help gatherings or studios committed to relationship dynamics and ADHD, and using assets, for example, books or online networks zeroed in on solid relationships for people with ADHD.

By recognizing and tending to these challenges, women with ADHD can foster a more profound comprehension of themselves and their remarkable qualities, cultivating more prominent self-sympathy and acknowledgment. Through successful correspondence, endeavors in association and using time productively, overseeing impulsivity, and looking for help, women with ADHD can pursue bu building better, additional satisfying relationships.

Chapter 6

Supportive Partnerships and Seeking Help

The Role of Partners in Supporting Women with ADHD

Partners assume an essential part in supporting women with ADHD, as their comprehension and backing can significantly influence the well-being and progress of the relationship. By perceiving the special challenges faced by women with ADHD and effectively captivating in steady systems, partners can establish a climate that encourages a solid and flourishing relationship.

One vital part of supporting women with ADHD is creating sympathy and understanding. Partners can teach themselves about ADHD, its side effects, and how it appears in women. This understanding assists partners with perceiving that specific ways of behaving or challenges experienced by their partner are not deliberate or individual, but rather connected with ADHD. By compassionately recognizing these difficulties, partners can make a safe and non-critical space for open communication and common help.

Powerful communication is fundamental in any relationship, including those with ADHD. partners can effectively pay attention to their partner's considerations and sentiments, approving their encounters and effectively captivating the discussion. This can assist women with ADHD to feel appreciated and esteemed, upgrading intimate closeness inside the relationship.

Steady partners can likewise help with commonsense procedures to address ADHD-related difficulties. They can team up in arranging undertakings, making frameworks for updates or cutoff times, and laying out schedules that advance construction and association. By offering support in regions where their partner might battle, partners can mitigate pressure and decrease the effects of ADHD side effects on day-to-day existence.

Consolation and inspiration are useful assets in supporting women with ADHD. Partners can offer uplifting feedback and commend their partner's accomplishments, regardless of how little they might appear. This cultivates a feeling of achievement and lifts self-assurance, which can be instrumental in

overseeing ADHD side effects and keeping up with inspiration.

Besides, partners can assume a part in assisting women with ADHD to keep focused on their treatment plans. This can include reminding them to take prescriptions, going to treatment meetings together, or investigating and figuring out different treatment choices. By effectively taking part in their partner's ADHD the board, partners show their responsibility and backing, engaging women with ADHD to focus on their prosperity.

In conclusion, partners sought to focus on self-care and look for help for themselves. Being involved with somebody with ADHD can be trying on occasion, and partners actually must address their necessities and look for assets or treatment if fundamental. Dealing with one's own psychological and intimate well-being guarantees that partners can give the comprehension and backing required for an effective relationship.

All in all, partners play a crucial part in supporting women with ADHD. By developing sympathy, rehearsing viable correspondence, executing commonsense procedures, offering support, and focusing on self-care, partners can establish a

climate that advances grasping, development, and strength inside the relationship. Through a cooperative and strong methodology, partners can assist women with ADHD explore the challenges they face and flourish in their social excursion.

Open Communication and Joint Effort in Relationships

Open communication and joint effort inside relationships are indispensable perspectives for women with ADHD to develop solid and fruitful associations.

Open communication includes establishing a climate where the two partners have a solid sense of reassurance, heard, and regarded. It involves being transparent about considerations, sentiments, and concerns, in this manner cultivating straightforwardness and trust. For women with ADHD, open communication permits them to communicate their interesting difficulties, share their requirements, and look for understanding from their partner. It creates a strong climate, lessening the feeling of separation that can accompany living with ADHD.

Coordinated effort, then again, includes cooperating to explore the effect of ADHD on the relationship. It requires the two partners to effectively partake in critical thinking, navigation, and tracking down serviceable arrangements. Coordinated effort recognizes that ADHD influences two people and perceives the significance of shared liability regarding dealing with its impacts on the relationship. Women with ADHD can profit from coordinated efforts by looking for information and understanding from their partners, utilizing their assets, and offering help in regions where they might battle.

By encouraging open communication and cooperation in relationships, women with ADHD can encounter a few advantages. It, first and foremost, advances getting it and compassion, assisting their joining forces with better appreciating the challenges related to ADHD. This prompts expanded tolerance, and support, and decreased disappointment in the relationship. Moreover, open communication and cooperation take into consideration the advancement of methodologies and frameworks that take care of the extraordinary requirements of women with ADHD. Through open

discourse, couples can examine and execute useful answers to oversee ADHD side effects, for example, laying out schedules, using updates, or making hierarchical frameworks customized to the singular's inclinations and assets.

Besides, open communication and coordinated effort act as an establishment for critical thinking. Couples can straightforwardly talk about moves that emerge because of ADHD and work together to track down intelligent fixes. By including the two partners in the critical thinking process, women with ADHD feel appreciated and approved, while their partners gain a more profound comprehension of their encounters.

Besides, a cooperative methodology assists with circulating liabilities and keeps the weight from exclusively falling on the lady with ADHD. Partners can share errands, delegate liabilities, and guarantee a fair appropriation of family tasks, nurturing obligations, and different responsibilities. This decreases overpower and permits women with ADHD to zero in on their assets, hence cultivating a more adjusted and amicable relationship.

In outline, open communication and cooperation are urgent for women with ADHD in supporting solid relationships. By making an air of understanding,

effectively including the two partners in critical thinking, and sharing liabilities, couples can construct serious areas of strength for help, understanding, and collaboration. Through these practices, women with ADHD can flourish and develop relationships that are both satisfying and effectively explore the challenges related to ADHD.

Finding Professional Support and Resources for Strengthening Relationships

Finding professional support and resources for strengthening relationships is a fundamental stage in enabling women with ADHD to explore their extraordinary challenges and cultivate sound associations. Professional support can give priceless direction, methodologies, and bits of knowledge customized explicitly to the necessities of women with ADHD, assisting them with building more grounded, additional satisfying relationships.

One vital road for looking for professional help is through treatment or direction. By working with a certified specialist who has some expertise in ADHD or relationships, women can take part in a protected and strong climate where they can

investigate their encounters, feelings, and relationship designs. Advisors can offer customized mediation, like mental conduct treatment (CBT) or persuasive conduct treatment (DBT), that addresses center ADHD side effects, intimate guidelines, relational abilities, and compromise. Notwithstanding treatment, support gatherings can likewise be useful for women with ADHD. These gatherings furnish a valuable chance to interface with other people who share comparable encounters, considering a feeling of approval and shared learning. Support gatherings might be worked with by experts or composed of companions who can share important experiences, systems, and assets, giving a feeling of local area and consolation.

While looking for professional support, it is essential to consider the qualifications and experience of the people or associations offering the help. Search for experts who work in ADHD, relationships, or both, as they will have a more profound comprehension of the particular challenges faced by women with ADHD in their relationships.

It may very well be useful to ask about their preparation, confirmations, and ability to guarantee that they are prepared to give the best help.

Moreover, online assets and legitimate sites can be brilliant wellsprings of data and backing. Numerous associations and specialists offer articles, sites, digital broadcasts, and online courses explicitly customized to ADHD and relationships. These assets can give important experiences, reasonable exhortation, and apparatuses for further developing relationship dynamics, correspondence, and generally speaking prosperity. Be that as it may, it is vital to fundamentally assess the validity and unwavering quality of online sources to guarantee the data given is proof-based and reliable.

In conclusion, feel free to contact your medical care supplier or therapist who represents considerable authority in ADHD. They can furnish references to experts with ability in relationships and ADHD, ordeal direction on getting to suitable assets.

In rundown, finding proficient help and assets for reinforcing relationships is critical for women with ADHD. Whether through treatment, support gatherings, online assets, or medical services experts, looking for a particular direction can enable women to comprehend and address their novel difficulties, foster successful techniques for

exploring relationships, and at last develop better and additional satisfying associations.

Chapter 7

Keeping up with Boundaries and Self-Support

Significance of Defining and Keeping up with Individual Boundaries

Defining and keeping up with individual boundaries is essential for women with ADHD as it lays out a healthy identity regard, jams profound well-being, and advances better relationships. ADHD can make it try to oversee time, feelings, and impulsivity, frequently making women battle with confidence and keeping up with command over their own space. By defining boundaries, women with ADHD can characterize their cutoff points and convey their requirements. This enables them to focus on their well-being and forestall overstretching themselves in relationships. Boundaries go about as a defensive safeguard, keeping others from exploiting their time, energy, and feelings. For women with ADHD, keeping up with individual boundaries can assist with directing their impulsivity and indiscreet dynamic inclinations. It permits them to stop,

reflect, and settle on smart decisions, as opposed to following up on prompt longings or tensions from others. Thus, they can stay away from incautious ways of behaving that might prompt unfortunate results or stressed relationships. Boundaries likewise play a crucial part in saving profound prosperity. Women with ADHD frequently have increased awareness and may encounter profound overpowering more strongly than others. Defining boundaries can assist with controlling profound reactions and forestall intimate burnout. It empowers women to lay out sound intimate space, permitting them to re-energize, process their sentiments, and impart their necessities without feeling overpowered or consumed by the feelings of others.

In relationships, boundaries give clarity and layout common regard between people. They assist women with ADHD in maintaining a good overall arrangement between their necessities and the requirements of others. By plainly characterizing boundaries, thcy can convey their cutoff points to partners, companions, and relatives, forestalling sensations of disdain or being underestimated. This encourages better and additional satisfying relationships based on trust and regard.

Also, defining and keeping up with individual boundaries encourages self-backing. It enables women to advocate for their necessities, focus on self-care, and pursue decisions lined up with their qualities and objectives. It permits them to stand up for themselves without hesitation, offer their viewpoints, and pursue choices that help their general prosperity. This reinforces their healthy identity and lifts self-assurance, the two of which are significant for exploring existence with ADHD.

Eventually, boundaries go about as a type of self-care for women with ADHD, guaranteeing their necessities are met and their psychological and intimate well-being is secured. By laying out and upholding individual boundaries, they can make a steady system that guides them in dealing with their ADHD side effects and keeping up with sound relationships. It is a fundamental part of self-strengthening and self-improvement for women with ADHD, empowering them to flourish and lead satisfying lives.

Empathicness Abilities for Self-Support and Keeping up with Deference

Empathic abilities for self-support and keeping up with deference are indispensable apparatuses for women with ADHD to explore relationships really and guarantee their requirements are met.

Women with ADHD frequently face moves in articulating their thoughts emphatically because of impulsivity, low confidence, and trouble dealing with feelings. Nonetheless, creating self-assuredness abilities can engage them to convey their considerations, sentiments, and boundaries consciously and clearly.

Self-promotion includes supporting one and effectively affirming one's privileges, needs and wants. For women with ADHD, it implies perceiving their assets, figuring out their difficulties, and unhesitatingly communicating them to other people. This could incorporate conveying their favored communication styles, defining boundaries, or mentioning facilities in private or expert settings. Keeping up with deference is a fundamental part of decisiveness abilities. It includes communicating one's thoughts in a manner that advances transparent communication while thinking about the sentiments and points of view of others. Women with ADHD can learn systems to communicate their necessities and perspectives without being excessively forceful or detached, tracking down an equilibrium that encourages sound relationships and shared understanding.

Creating confidence abilities and keeping up with deference takes practice and self-reflection. A few procedures that can be useful include:

Mindfulness: Grasping one's sentiments, wants, and boundaries are pivotal before powerful communication can happen. Considering individual qualities, qualities, and necessities can assist women with ADHD gain lucidity and trust in putting themselves out there decisively.

Undivided Attention: Compelling communication includes putting oneself out there as well as listening mindfully to other people. Undivided attention permits women with ADHD to grasp alternate points of view and approve of the sentiments and perspectives of others, advancing a deferential discourse.

"I" Explanations: Utilizing "I" proclamations conveys considerations and sentiments without accusing or censuring others. For instance, rather than saying, "You generally hinder me," a more empathic methodology would be, "I feel baffled when I'm intruded on during our discussions."

Defining and Keeping up with Boundaries: Boundary setting is urgent for self-care and keeping up with solid relationships. women with ADHD can impart their cutoff points and assumptions while supporting them reliably. This enables them to focus on their well-being and guarantee their necessities are regarded.

Certainty-Building Methods: Building confidence and certainty is fundamental for rehearsing emphaticness. Women with ADHD can chip away at positive self-talk, recognizing their assets and achievements, and looking for valuable chances to rehearse emphaticness in strong conditions.

Compromise: Struggle is unavoidable when seeing someone, however, it very well may be drawn nearer decisively and consciously. Women with ADHD can learn systems like undivided attention, splitting the difference, and finding shared benefit answers for address clashes helpfully.

Eventually, creating empathic abilities for self-support and keeping up with deference enables women with ADHD to have a voice in their relationships. By successfully communicating their requirements, boundaries, and perspectives while considering the viewpoints of others, they can encourage better and additional satisfying associations with people around them.

Building an Encouraging Group of People and Getting Assets for Extra Assistance

Building an encouraging group of people and getting assets for extra assistance is critical for women with ADHD to successfully deal with their condition and flourish in their relationships and day-to-day routines. ADHD can bring remarkable challenges and it's vital to encircle yourself with understanding and steady people who can give direction, consolation, and functional help.

One method for building an encouraging group of people is by searching out similar people who can connect with your encounters. Consider joining support bunches explicitly customized for women with ADHD, both on the web and face-to-face.

These gatherings give a place of refuge to share battles, trade survival techniques, and proposition important bits of knowledge from other people who have confronted comparable difficulties. Peer backing can be hugely soothing and enabling, as it guarantees you that you are in good company on your excursion.

Notwithstanding peer support, proficient assistance with canning assumes a vital part in overseeing ADHD. It is fitting to counsel a medical services professional, for example, a therapist or clinician, who has practical experience in ADHD. They can give precise findings, offer customized treatment plans, and guide you through the course of medicine, treatment, or a mix of both. These experts can likewise assist you with exploring any existing together circumstances, for example, nervousness or sadness, which are generally found close to ADHD. Moreover, instructive assets are promptly accessible to assist you with better grasping ADHD and foster compelling systems for overseeing it. Books, articles, and sites committed to ADHD can give significant data and useful methods for overseeing side effects, further developing association, and improving relational abilities. Also, web recordings and online courses facilitated by specialists in the field can offer further bits of knowledge and direction.

One more significant part of building an encouraging group of people is including your friends and family. Teaching your partner, relatives, and dear companions about ADHD can cultivate understanding and compassion. They can find out about the remarkable challenges you face, and together, you can investigate ways of meeting your requirements and establishing a steady climate. Open communication with your friends and family is critical in laying out an organization of understanding and help.

Ultimately, recall that looking for help is certainly not an indication of a shortcoming but an indication of solidarity and self-care. Perceive that you merit and are qualified for access to the assets and backing accessible to you. By effectively searching out an encouraging group of people and using accessible assets, you are making an enabling stride toward dealing with your ADHD really and building a satisfying life.

In rundown, constructing an encouraging group of people and getting extra assets give women with

ADHD the essential devices to effectively explore their condition. Through peer support, proficient direction, instructive materials, and comprehensive communication with friends and family, women with ADHD can track down figuring out, help, and a climate that encourages their development and prosperity. Keep in mind, you are in good company, and with the right help, you can flourish and lead a satisfying life notwithstanding the challenges presented by ADHD.

Chapter 8

Cultivating a Healthy Lifestyle

Addressing the Impact of Nutrition and Physical Activity on ADHD Symptoms

Nutrition and physical activity play a critical part in our general prosperity, and they can likewise significantly affect overseeing ADHD side effects in women. With regards to tending to ADHD, taking on a comprehensive methodology that incorporates a reasonable eating routine and standard activity can upgrade the center, mental capability, and state of mind security.

Adjusted Diet: A nutritious, adjusted diet plentiful in nutrients, minerals, and fundamental supplements is crucial for women with ADHD. Certain supplements have been found to help cerebrum wellbeing, further develop fixation, and direct mindset. Instances of helpful supplements include:

Omega-3 Unsaturated Fats: Tracked down in greasy fish, flaxseeds, and pecans, omega-3 unsaturated fats can work on mental capability and lessen the side effects of ADHD.

Protein: Including lean proteins like chicken, fish, beans, and tofu manages dopamine and norepinephrine levels, which assume a part in consideration and concentration.

Complex Starches: Decide on entire grains, organic products, and vegetables, which discharge energy gradually, keeping up with stable glucose levels and supporting the supported center.

Cell reinforcements: Food varieties wealthy in cell reinforcements, like berries, mixed greens, and bright natural products, can assist with diminishing aggravation and oxidative pressure in the cerebrum, possibly further developing ADHD side effects.

Keeping away from Triggers: A few people with ADHD might have responsive qualities or sensitivity to specific food varieties or added substances, like counterfeit tones, flavors, or additives. Recognizing and staying away from these triggers can assist with overseeing ADHD side effects all the more successfully.

Ordinary Activity: Taking part in standard actual work has been displayed to have various advantages for people with ADHD, including further developed

fixation, motivation control, and state-of-mind guidelines. This is the way exercise can decidedly affect ADHD side effects:

Expanded Dopamine: Exercise supports the creation of dopamine, a synapse related to inspiration and prize, which can assist with further developing concentration and consideration.

Upgraded Leader Capability: Active work animates the prefrontal cortex, the region of the mind liable for navigation, arranging, and motivation control. This can prompt better association and self-guideline.

Stress Decrease: Exercise discharges endorphins, the "vibe great" chemicals that can mitigate pressure, nervousness, and sadness, and normal co-happening conditions with ADHD.

Further Developed Rest: Customary activity advances better rest quality and length, which is significant for overseeing ADHD side effects and keeping up with by and large prosperity.

It's essential to take note that while sustenance and active work can be useful in overseeing ADHD side effects, they are not independent medicines. They ought to be consolidated as a component of an extensive ADHD executives plan, which might

incorporate treatment, drugs, and other strong systems.

Integrating a decent eating routine and customary activity into your way of life might require a change and trial and error to find what turns out best for you. Talking with a medical care proficient or an enlisted dietitian can give customized direction and suggestions custom-made to your particular necessities.

By tending to the effect of sustenance and actual work on ADHD side effects, women with ADHD can enable themselves to assume command over their well-being and streamline their general work. With a comprehensive methodology that supports both the body and brain, women can more readily deal with their side effects, increase concentration, and efficiency, and upgrade their general personal satisfaction.

Rest Cleanliness and its Effect on Intimate Well-Being

Rest cleanliness alludes to a bunch of pursues and routines that advance sound rest designs. For women with ADHD, keeping up with great rest and

cleanliness is of most extreme significance as it can essentially influence their profound well-being.

Satisfactory and soothing rest, right off the bat, is critical for overseeing ADHD side effects successfully. Lack of sleep can compound side effects like impulsivity, hyperactivity, and negligence, making it harder to concentrate, concentrate, and direct feelings. By focusing on reliable and quality rest, women with ADHD can work on their general consideration and chief working, prompting better profound guidelines and by and large well-being.

Moreover, rest assumes an essential part in profound handling and guidelines. During rest, the mind solidifies recollections, processes feelings, and reestablishes energy levels. Sufficient rest considers the fruitful handling and mix of everyday encounters, decreasing the profound burden conveyed into the following day. Then again, constant lack of sleep can uplift intimate reactivity, making it more difficult for women with ADHD to oversee pressure, clashes, or extreme feelings in their relationships.

Laying out sound rest cleanliness rehearses includes taking on a normal rest plan, holding back nothing

sleep time and wake-up time. Making an unwinding pre-sleep time standard, for example, participating in quieting exercises like perusing or cleaning up, can flag the body and brain that now is the ideal time to slow down and plan for rest. Establishing an agreeable rest climate: utilizing a strong sleeping cushion and pads, guaranteeing a dull and calm room, and keeping electronic gadgets out of the room to limit distractions is likewise helpful.

Also, keeping away from energizers like caffeine and nicotine near sleep time can assist with advancing better rest quality. Participating in standard actual work during the day, yet staying away from enthusiastic activity near sleep time, can add to a more serene night's rest. Laying out a steady wind-down daily schedule and rehearsing unwinding strategies, like profound breathing or contemplation, can likewise support progressing to a quiet state before rest.

Finally, it is fundamental to lay out a good arrangement between private obligations and rest needs. women with ADHD frequently have occupied lives and may battle with focusing on self-care, including rest. In any case, perceiving the basic job of rest in intimate well-being can assist

with moving needs and change timetables to consider adequate rest.

By rehearsing great rest cleanliness, women with ADHD can further develop their intimate well-being by decreasing side effects, upgrading profound guidelines, and advancing in general mental and actual well-being. Focusing on quality rest sets the establishment for a better, more healthy lifestyle and better exploring the challenges of overseeing ADHD in day-to-day existence and relationships.

Incorporating Care and Unwinding Procedures for General Well-Being

Coordinating care and unwinding strategies for by and large well-being of ADHD includes taking on unambiguous practices that advance tranquility, mindfulness, and further developed centers. women with ADHD frequently face increased degrees of stress, tension, and challenges with fixation. By integrating care and unwinding procedures into their day-to-day schedules, they can develop a more prominent feeling of intimate prosperity, decrease the side effects of ADHD, and upgrade their general personal satisfaction.

Care alludes to the act of deliberately concentrating on the current second, without judgment. For women with ADHD, care activities can assist with pointing out their prompt insight, permitting them to turn out to be more mindful of their viewpoints, feelings, and actual sensations. This mindfulness empowers them to perceive and oversee interruptions all the more really, prompting further developed fixation and efficiency.

Unwinding strategies assume a significant part in lessening feelings of anxiety, which is especially significant for women with ADHD. Ongoing pressure can fuel ADHD side effects, making it trying to oversee impulsivity, control feelings, and keep a feeling of quiet. By integrating unwinding strategies like profound breathing activities, moderate muscle unwinding, or directed symbolism, women with ADHD can initiate their body's unwinding reaction and check the adverse consequences of stress. These practices advance a condition of profound unwinding, calming both the psyche and the body, and considering a feeling of serenity and revival.

By coordinating care and unwinding methods into their day-to-day routines, women with ADHD can encounter a few advantages. These include:

Further Developed Concentration and Consideration: Care practices train the psyche to remain present, lessening interruption and upgrading the capacity to keep up with center-around tasks.

Stress Decrease: Unwinding methods enact the body's unwinding reaction, balancing the adverse consequences of weight on ADHD side effects. Lower feelings of anxiety take into consideration working on intimate guidelines and a more noteworthy feeling of general prosperity.

Improved Mindfulness: Care rehearses develop a more profound comprehension of one's viewpoints, feelings, and personal conduct standards. This mindfulness can assist women with ADHD to perceive and oversee side effects all the more.

Further Developed Motivation Control: Care upgrades the capacity to stop and answer deliberately, lessening indiscreet ways of behaving normally connected with ADHD.

Better Intimate Guideline: By tuning into present-second encounters, women with ADHD can

foster abilities to successfully perceive and manage their feelings more.

Expanded Flexibility: Care and unwinding practices assemble strength, empowering women to explore challenges and mishaps with no sweat and versatility.

To coordinate care and unwinding strategies into their lives, women with ADHD can take part in practices, for example,

Careful Relaxing: Requiring a couple of moments every day to zero in on the breath, noticing its cadence and sensations, can assist with securing the brain and advance a feeling of quiet.

Body Check Reflection: By efficiently focusing on various locales of the body, from head to toe, women can develop a more profound association with their bodies and delivery pressure.

Careful Development: Participating in exercises like yoga, kendo, or strolling reflection can join actual development with care, advancing physical and mental unwinding.

Directed Symbolism: Paying attention to or picturing positive and quiet scenes can move the brain to a quiet mental scene, lessening pressure and advancing unwinding.

Moderate Muscle Unwinding: By straining and afterward loosening up various muscle bunches all through the body, women can deliver actual pressure and prompt a condition of profound unwinding.

Care in Day-to-Day Exercises: Integrating care into routine exercises, like eating, washing dishes, or strolling, can secure regard for the current second and diminish dissipated thinking.

By and large, coordinating care and unwinding methods into the existence of women with ADHD can give important instruments to overseeing side effects, decreasing pressure, and advancing generally speaking well-being and prosperity. With ordinary practice, these procedures can engage women with ADHD to develop a more noteworthy feeling of harmony, concentration, and flexibility, permitting them to flourish in their regular day-to-day existences and relationships.

Chapter 9

Thriving in Intimate Relationships and Beyond

Strategies for Nurturing Romantic Relationships with ADHD

Strategies for nurturing romantic relationships with ADHD include carrying out unambiguous strategies and practices to advance grasping, sympathy, and successful communication between partners. ADHD, or Attention-Deficit/Hyperactivity Disorder, can remarkably affect relationships, making it vital to foster techniques that address the challenges and expand the qualities of the two partners included.

Training and Mindfulness: Start by instructing the two partners about ADHD, its side effects, and its expected effect on relationships. Understanding the manners by which ADHD appears in day-to-day existence can cultivate compassion and decrease mistaken assumptions. It assists in perceiving that ADHD is a neurological condition, and its related side effects like impulsivity, carelessness, and trouble with the association are not deliberate.

Transparent Correspondence: Lay out areas of strength for transparent communication inside the relationship. Make a place of refuge where the two partners can communicate their necessities, concerns, and battles without judgment. Empower undivided attention and approve of each other's encounters. Consistently address any errors or clashes before they arise.

Lay out Schedules and Construction: ADHD can make it trying to keep up with design and schedules, which are significant for security in relationships. Cooperate to make timetables, schedules, and suggestions to assist with day-to-day errands, shared liabilities, and significant occasions. Carry out hierarchical instruments and frameworks that take special care of the two partners' requirements, guaranteeing that significant data is effectively open and that undertakings are circulated decently.

Put Aside Quality Time: Devote quality opportunities to support the intimate association inside the relationship. Plan exercises that the two partners appreciate and try to participate in significant discussions and shared encounters. This quality time reinforces the connection among partners and diminishes the strain that

ADHD-related challenges might put on the relationship.

Strong Climate: Establish a steady climate that recognizes and obliges the challenges presented by ADHD. This incorporates giving support, offering help when required, and showing restraint toward one another's separate battles. Practice sympathy and shun faulting or reprimanding your partner for ADHD-related hardships.

Look for Proficient Assistance if Necessary: Consider looking for direction from experts who have some expertise in ADHD and relationships. Couples treatment or relationship training can give significant bits of knowledge, instruments, and procedures custom-made to your particular circumstance. A prepared proficient person can assist you with exploring difficulties, further developing relational abilities, and fostering survival strategies that fortify your relationship.

Keep up with Self-Care: Urge the two partners to focus on self-care, as people with ADHD might encounter more significant levels of pressure or dissatisfaction. Keeping up with individual well-being takes into consideration a better and seriously satisfying organization. This incorporates

getting sufficient rest, participating in normal activity, rehearsing pressure the executive's methods, and seeking after private interests and leisure activities.

Celebrate and Use Qualities: Perceive and praise the qualities of the joint forces with ADHD. People with ADHD frequently have exceptional characteristics like inventiveness, immediacy, and deep unboundary energy. Embrace and value these characteristics, as they can be instrumental in giving pleasure and fervor to the relationship.

Adaptability and Versatility: Comprehend that adaptability and flexibility are urgent when seeing someone with ADHD. Assumptions and plans might be changed on occasion because of the erratic idea of ADHD side effects. Being understanding and obliging during these occasions can fundamentally decrease pressure and rub inside the relationship.

Persistence and Absolution: ADHD can some of the time lead to botches, missed arrangements, or ncglcct. Practice tolerance and pardoning when these circumstances happen. Recollecting that nobody is great, and recognizing this can make a more sympathetic and forgiving environment in the relationship.

By carrying out these procedures, couples can establish a climate that cultivates figuring out, empathy, and development. At last, sustaining a heartfelt connection with ADHD includes embracing the challenges while valuing the extraordinary qualities that the two people bring to the organization.

Adjusting Individual Objectives and Aggregate Development

Adjusting individual objectives and aggregate development for women with ADHD is tied in with tracking down a solid balance between seeking after private yearnings and sustaining the relationships in their lives. women with ADHD frequently have novel gifts, interests, and aspirations that drive them to seek after their objectives, dreams, and self-awareness. Simultaneously, it is fundamental to perceive that relationships assume a critical part in their general well-being and joy. Recognizing the significance of aggregate development implies effective financial planning time, exertion, and energy into building and sustaining associations

with their partners, relatives, companions, and friends and family.

To work out some kind of harmony, women with ADHD can begin by distinguishing and conveying their singular objectives and goals. This includes grasping their interests, interests, and what genuinely satisfies them. By defining clear objectives and boundaries, they can travel toward self-improvement and accomplish the feeling of achievement they want. All the while, it is essential to encourage correspondence, joint effort, and backing inside their relationships. This involves effectively captivating their partners, relatives, friends, and family to figure out their requirements, wants, and goals. By effectively tuning in, showing compassion, and offering help, women with ADHD can establish a climate where aggregate development is sustained and celebrated.

Women with ADHD can likewise investigate tracking down shared objectives and interests inside their relationships. This could include distinguishing normal side interests, exercises, or causes that they can seek after together, encouraging association and a feeling of harmony.

Adjusting individual objectives and aggregate development requires transparent communication with the critical individuals in their lives. By communicating their cravings and desires, and effectively paying attention to the requirements of their partners, relatives, and companions, women with ADHD can establish a cooperative climate where both individual and aggregate development are esteemed. It is critical to recall that finding this equilibrium isn't simple all the time. Women with ADHD might experience challenges like impulsivity, carelessness, or battles with time usage that can influence their capacity to meet their singular objectives or add to aggregate development. In any case, by using procedures like setting reasonable assumptions, utilizing compelling time-usage methods, and looking for help when required, it becomes conceivable to explore these challenges and keep advancing toward individual and social development.

At last, adjusting individual objectives and aggregate development for women with ADHD is tied in with tracking down amiability and satisfaction in the two parts of their lives. It includes perceiving the worth of self-awareness while

likewise putting resources into the relationships that give pleasure, association, and backing. By embracing their assets, looking for understanding, and encouraging open correspondence, women with ADHD can find an agreeable mix that considers individual satisfaction and the improvement of significant and flourishing relationships.

Embracing Self-Esteem and Self-Acknowledgment on the Excursion toward Flourishing Relationships

Embracing self-esteem and self-acknowledgement is a key part of encouraging flourishing relationships for women with ADHD. It includes fostering a profound feeling of empathy, understanding, and appreciation for oneself, including the exceptional characteristics, difficulties, and qualities related to ADHD. Women with ADHD frequently face hardships in relationships because of the side effects and attributes of their condition. They might battle with impulsivity, neglect, unfortunately using time effectively, and trouble putting together contemplations and errands. These challenges can in

some cases lead to identity uncertainty, dissatisfaction, and negative self-discernment.

In any case, by embracing confidence and self-acknowledgement, women with ADHD can develop a better mentality and way to deal with relationships. It starts with perceiving that ADHD isn't a blemish or boundary, but rather a piece of what their identity is. It includes recognizing that everybody has their assets and shortcomings, and ADHD is only one part of their one-of-a-kind personality. Self-esteem and self-acknowledgement enable women with ADHD to be kinder to themselves, pardon their slip-ups, and zero in on their assets and achievements. It is tied in with embracing their distinction and understanding that they deserve love, regard, and significant associations, despite the challenges they might confront.

By rehearsing self-esteem, women with ADHD can foster a positive mental self-portrait and construct trust in their capacities. This recently discovered self-acknowledgement empowers them to convey their necessities successfully and decisively, put down sensible stopping points, and keep a good arrangement in relationships. It likewise permits

them to advocate for their well-being and look for help when required. Flourishing relationships require an underpinning of confidence and self-acknowledgement. At the point when women with ADHD embrace themselves completely, they make space for development, understanding, and legitimacy in their associations with others. They can straightforwardly convey their battles and assets with their partners, cultivating sympathy, empathy, and shared help.

Self-esteem and self-acknowledgement likewise furnish a focal point through which women with ADHD can explore challenges and mishaps with flexibility and self-compassion. Instead of incorporating disappointments or mishaps as private inadequacies, they can see them as any open doors for development and getting the hang of, building their versatility and assurance to defeat snags along with their partners.

At last, embracing self-esteem and self-acknowledgement is a deep rooted venture that engages women with ADHD to make satisfying and flourishing relationships. It permits them to perceive their value, praise their accomplishments, and encourage authentic associations in light of figuring

out, backing, and love. By sustaining a positive relationship with themselves, women with ADHD can emanate certainty, validness, and self-assuredness, draw
ing in solid relationships that upgrade their general prosperity.

Conclusion

Embracing Your Assets and Building Solid, Enduring Associations with ADHD

Thinking About Self-Improvement and Progress

Thinking about Self-Improvement and progress is an urgent part of the excursion for women with ADHD. It includes making a stride back, stopping, and deliberately inspecting one's encounters, accomplishments, and areas of progress.

For women with ADHD, this cycle fills different needs. It, right off the bat, considers a more profound comprehension of oneself, empowering the ID and affirmation of individual qualities, gifts, and strength. Thinking about self-improvement gives a chance to praise the achievements accomplished en route, regardless of how huge or little they might appear. It assists people with valuing their extraordinary characteristics, achievements, and the headway they have made regardless of the challenges presented by ADHD.

In addition, considering self-improvement and progress enables women with ADHD to distinguish regions in which they have improved or conquered impediments. This mindfulness is priceless, as it considers the acknowledgment of techniques and survival strategies that have demonstrated power. By recognizing these positive changes, women can acquire certainty and inspiration to additionally create and refine their adapting abilities.

Also, reflection empowers the acknowledgment of regions that might in any case require consideration and development. It urges people to take on an empathetic and non-critical methodology, understanding that self-improvement is a continuous cycle. By distinguishing regions that need improvement, women with ADHD can search for extra help, assets, or systems to address those particular difficulties. Considering self-awareness and progress likewise assists women with ADHD keep a positive mentality. It fills in as an update that progress is conceivable and that misfortunes don't characterize their capacities or potential. Through self-improvement, they can reevaluate misfortunes by gaining open doors and tracking down motivation from past achievements.

Besides, thinking about self-improvement and progress creates a feeling of strengthening and organization. It builds up the idea that people with ADHD can assume command over their lives and roll out certain improvements. It advises them that they can shape their story and conquer the challenges related to ADHD.

In outline, thinking about self-improvement and progress is an imperative practice for women with ADHD. It considers self-appreciation, the recognizable proof of viable systems, the affirmation of regions still needing improvement, the support of a positive mentality, and the strengthening to assume responsibility for one's excursion. By taking part in this cycle, women with ADHD can develop a more noteworthy identity certainty, versatility, and general prosperity.

Support and Inspiration for Proceeded Progress

Support and inspiration are significant parts of making progress for women with ADHD. It is critical to comprehend that living with ADHD can introduce interesting difficulties, however it doesn't characterize your value or potential. With the right

procedures and outlook, you can conquer deterrents and flourish in all aspects of your life.

It right off the bat, is fundamental to perceive and praise your achievements, regardless of how little they might appear. ADHD can frequently cause errands to feel overpowering or challenging to finish, so recognizing and commending your accomplishments can help your certainty and give the inspiration to continue to push forward.

Moreover, putting forth sensible objectives is vital to keeping up with energy and progress. Separate bigger undertakings into more modest, sensible advances, and spotlight on with extra care. Praise every achievement en route, building up your faith in your capacities and filling your inspiration to handle the following test.

Establishing a steady climate is likewise indispensable for proceeding with progress. Encircle yourself with people who comprehend and value your assets, while offering consolation and backing. Search out companions, family, or care groups who can give direction and sympathy during testing times. Offering encounters to other people who have confronted comparable obstacles can be moving and

assist you with remaining inspired on your excursion.

Moreover, fostering a standard that works for you is fundamental. Integrate procedures like breaking undertakings into more modest lumps, using visual guides or updates, and laying out an organized timetable. By setting reliable schedules, you create a feeling of consistency and association, lessening pressure and expanding the center. At the point when you can depend on a solid daily practice, you are bound to remain spurred, keep up with energy, and accomplish your objectives.

One more compelling technique for keeping up with inspiration is to consistently survey your advancement and change on a case-by-case basis. Ponder your achievements, distinguish regions for development, and roll out fundamental improvements. This self-reflection permits you to praise your triumphs and recognize any potential hindrances to address proactively. By ceaselessly adjusting and gaining from your encounters, you can support inspiration and keep on advancing.

It is vital to recall that mishaps and challenges are a characteristic piece of any excursion. Rather than survey them as disappointments, view them as any

open doors for development and learning. Developing versatility and a positive outlook will assist you with returning quickly from mishaps and remaining spurred regardless of obstructions.

In conclusion, finding motivation through good examples of individual interests can light a fire inside you. Find people who have defeated comparative challenges, made progress, and gained from their accounts. Taking part in exercises that you are enthusiastic about can likewise give a feeling of satisfaction and motivation, filling your inspiration to succeed in all parts of your life.

In synopsis, support and inspiration for proceeding with progress for women with ADHD include perceiving and commending achievements, defining reasonable objectives, establishing a steady climate, laying out schedules, pondering headway and making changes, embracing challenges as learning valuable open doors and finding motivation through good examples and individual interests. By carrying out these techniques, you can keep up with your inspiration, defeat difficulties, and keep on making progress in your life regardless of living with ADHD.

Last Contemplations and Assets for Continuous Help and Development

In closing this guidel for sound relationships for women with ADHD, underscores the meaning of continuous help and self-awareness is significant. Keep in mind that overseeing ADHD and sustaining satisfying relationships is a continuous excursion that requires responsibility and self-compassion. Here are a few last considerations and significant assets to help you in your continuous development:

Observe Your Advancement: Pause for a minute to recognize your accomplishments and the headway you have made. Perceive that change requires some investment and exertion, and hail yourself for the means you have taken towards better relationships.

Practice Self-Care: Keep focusing on self-care as an imperative part of keeping up with in general prosperity. This incorporates normal activity, adequate rest, smart dieting, and taking part in exercises that give you pleasure and unwinding.

self-care reinforces your capacity to oversee ADHD side effects and cultivates flexibility inside relationships.

Look for Proceeded Training and Backing: Remain informed about the most recent examination, techniques, and assets accessible for overseeing ADHD in women. Go to studios, courses, or meetings connected with ADHD and relationship dynamics. Moreover, consider joining support gatherings or online networks explicitly intended for women with ADHD to interface with other people who share comparative encounters.

Proficient Help: Assuming that you feel overpowered or require extra direction, think about looking for proficient assistance. A psychological well-being proficient gaining practical experience in ADHD can give customized methodologies, adapting procedures, and treatment custom-made to your novel necessities. They can likewise offer direction in exploring relationship challenges and offer help for self-improvement.

Relationship Guiding: If you are in a serious relationship, couples directing can be massively useful. A prepared specialist can work with open correspondence, guide compromise, and help the two partners better get and back each other's necessities. Couples directing can reinforce the bond, advance compassion, and lay out a strong

starting point for a sound and flourishing relationship.

Remain Associated with Strong Partners: Keep up with open lines of communication with your partner, family, and companions. Share your encounters, difficulties, and wins with them. Take part in continuous exchanges about the effect of ADHD on your relationship and look for their comprehension and backing. Constructing and keeping areas of strength for an organization is fundamental for supported development and prosperity.

Extra Assets: The universe of ADHD assets is tremendous and consistently extending. Investigate books, digital broadcasts, sites, and gatherings devoted to ADHD and relationships. Instruct yourself on methodologies, strategies, and genuine encounters shared by others.

Keep in mind that you are in good company on this excursion. With mindfulness, self-care, and admittance to steady assets, you can construct and keep up with solid, satisfying relationships regardless of the challenges presented by ADHD. Remain committed, be thoughtful to yourself, and continue to take a stab at self-awareness and

association. You merit love, understanding, and bliss.

I have a Solicitation

Dear Readers,

I hope you liked "A Guide to Healthy Relationships for Women with ADHD" Your perspective matters a ton to me, and I'd very much want to hear your considerations.

Your review can truly help other people choose if this book is appropriate for them. Whether you partook in the substance, found the methods accommodating, or thought the data very much made sense, your bits of knowledge can rouse and direct individual readers. On the off chance that you have a couple of moments, I'd be thankful if you would compose a survey on stages like Goodreads, Amazon, or some other book survey site.

Your legitimate audits won't just assist me with improving but additionally inspire me to make more accommodating assets for individuals like you.

Gratitude for going along with me on this excursion, and I'm eager to hear your thought process about "A Guide to Healthy Relationships for Women with ADHD"

Your help implies a great deal!

All the best,
The Writer Meghan J. Brooks

Assuming you partook in that book and need more, I suggest looking at a portion of my different Books. You can track them down on my Author Central page on Amazon. Simply click the connection beneath:

https://www.amazon.com/author/meghanj.brookscounselor01